Lord, I Shall Be a House of Prayer!

Lord, I Shall Be a House of Prayer!

Developing a Relationship with Jesus

Toni Allen

Strategic Book Publishing and Rights Co.

Strategic Book Publishing & Rights Co., LLC
USA | Singapore
www.sbpra.net

For information about special discounts for bulk purchases, please contact Strategic Book Publishing and Rights Co. Special Sales, at bookorder@sbpra.net.

ISBN: 978-1-68235-275-5

DEDICATION

I give honor and glory to my Lord and Savior, Jesus Christ, for making my dream a reality. I dedicate this book to my beautiful daughter Destiny Ware, Lorenza Ware, my sister Monique Allen Story, Jayden Story, and Timothy Pernell whom I appreciate and dearly love.

This book was inspired by the Holy Spirit and dedicated to every person who desires a deeper relationship with our Lord and Savior, Jesus Christ. God wants His people to know that He loves them and He wants us to have a sincere desire for Him, not for the benefits, but to pursue Him for a loving, committed relationship. Prayer unlocks and unleashes all God has for us. God wants us to know that He is not some far-out deity in outer space. He is at the door of each of our hearts, waiting for us to invite Him in.

"Am I a God at hand, saith the Lord, and not a God afar off?"
(Jeremiah 23;23)

After reading this book,
"YOU SHALL BE A HOUSE OF PRAYER!"

ACKNOWLEDGMENTS

Lynn and the team at Strategic Book Publishing and Rights Agency, for your confidence to take on this project. I pray that God continues to bless you and your team beyond your expectations.

Friends and Family: Thank you to all who supported and encouraged me through this journey. Thank you for every encouraging word, every prayer and every seed that was sown into my life to keep me moving forward. I pray that God will continue to bless you beyond measure and grant you your heart's desire as you grow in Him.

TABLE OF CONTENTS

INTRODUCTION

Today, many books have been written on prayer. Obviously, the Lord is impressing prayer's importance upon us. The information in this book may not be new to many, but hopefully, it will be an encouragement and inspiration to increase your prayer life and to pray with vibrancy. The objective is to inspire all to want to pray, and to realize God loves you and desires to have an intimate relationship with you. This book is not offering false hope or empty promises, but providing you with biblical knowledge to grow in your relationship with God through prayer. I believe that one of the reasons many give up on praying is that they do not see their prayers answered and therefore they get angry with God. However, many prayers are unanswered because of a lack of a proper relationship with the Father. There are over 8000 promises in the Bible and all of them are available to God's children, as long as we are walking with Him in obedience.

Jesus is our role model as to how we should seek, obey, and have fellowship with God. We will take a look at Jesus's prayer life and see how we can emulate it, so we can also walk in the power of God.

Luke 11:1 begins, "One day Jesus was praying in a certain place. When he finished, one of his disciples said to him, 'Lord, teach us to pray just as John taught his disciples.'" Notice this passage doesn't say *"how"* to pray, but "to" pray, which is different. To pray suggests the desire to want to pray, which is the challenge.

1

So many people struggle with prayer; so many find it difficult to talk with God.

Many do not believe that they can communicate with the Creator of the Universe; many see our Creator as some deity far removed from themselves, so they only reach out to Him when they are in trouble. Some believe that only certain people can speak to God, while others do not make time to talk to God. Then there are those that do not realize or understand the importance of prayer. Why should all these hindrances and obstacles keep us from spending time with our loving Father?

My friend, do not be deceived. All of these are distractions and lies from Satan to keep you from recognizing and using your most powerful weapon. *PRAYER*. Your enemy knows the power in prayer, his goal is to keep you from knowing the power in prayer, and unfortunately, he has accomplished this objective in many of our lives. We as individuals, we as the church, have made prayer secondary or non-existent in our lives. But today we are serving notice to the Devil and all his demons that we are picking up our weapon to destroy all his works. It is Wartime, so pick up your weapon and let's go to battle.

A weapon is defined as something used to injure, defeat, or destroy—a means of gaining an advantage or defending oneself in conflict. We are definitely in a conflict with the Devil, but the good news is that Jesus has left us with a powerful weapon in our arsenal. Keep these definitions in mind as we gain more understanding and appreciation for prayer. Our goal is to take an offensive stance and dismantle Satan and his army's plots against us.

I am confident that after reading this book, you are going to have a greater desire to pray, a greater desire to hear the voice of our loving Father, and as a result a greater desire to accomplish His purpose in your life.

RIGHTS TO THE FAMILY INHERITANCE

In order to have access to the benefits promised, we must belong to the family of God. To belong to the family, you must place your faith in Jesus Christ. Throughout Scripture it is clear that God's ears are open to the repentant heart, and His ears are closed to the unjust and unrighteous **(John: 9:30, 1st Peter 3:12, Jeremiah 29:13 & Psalm 66:18).** This doesn't mean that He doesn't love the unjust or unrighteous. God loves all humanity, but, because of His perfect and holy nature, He will not and cannot tolerate sin. Because of His mercy, grace, compassion and goodness, He has made a way for all humanity to be freed from the power of sin and death. If you desire to have a relationship with the Father and experience Him in ways you never imagined, you must acknowledge, confess, and accept His only-begotten Son Jesus Christ as your Lord and Savior. **John 4:6** states that Jesus is the only way to the Father; no one comes to the Father but through Him. Everyone that calls upon the name of the Lord will be saved **(Romans 10:13).** If you are not sure you are saved, you may fast-forward to the end of the book and recite the repentance prayer. This book is not about salvation, but it's imperative that we understand that we must be saved and in the family of God to receive the many promises and provisions He has made to His children.

WHAT IS PRAYER?

Prayer is talking with God and listening to God. In the simplest form, it is a dialogue between you and God. Just as a natural relationship is built on strong effective communication, your relationship with the Father is built on strong and consistent communication. When you are trying to know more about someone, you engage in conversation with them. You talk to them, you ask them questions, you tell them how you feel, and they do likewise. This is setting the foundation for a relationship. In marriages or friendships, if there is poor or no communication, it will be a matter of time before the relationship goes south. Prayer is not something that we have to do; it is a privilege and honor to be able to communicate with the Creator of the Universe, the Creator of you and me. Through the blood of Jesus Christ, we have been reconciled to the Father, thus giving us the ability to enjoy fellowship with our Heavenly Father. We are no longer enemies to God—we are now His children. Don't take this for granted! Our God has invited us to speak with Him and He promised that He will answer. In **Jeremiah 29:12**, God says, "Then ye shall call upon me, and ye shall go pray unto me, and I will hearken unto you." Let this penetrate into your spirit! Imagine, little you, little me, made from the dust of the earth, have been invited by Almighty God to talk with Him.

In order to have an effective prayer life, you must be on speaking terms with God. In other words, you must be in relationship with Him. I am not referring to drive-by prayers, occasionally dropping by when things are not going right, or your way, or when you need something. I am talking about constantly and consistently talking to the Father on a regular basis. Prayer has become your lifestyle. You are living the lifestyle declared in **1st Thessalonians 5:16,** praying without ceasing. Obviously, we cannot spend 24-7 on our knees, (and that is not what this passage of scripture is suggesting) but we can work towards developing and having a prayerful attitude and heart position at all times. This is not to substitute the quiet scheduled time we definitely need with the Lord; this should be an extension, an outgrowth of that quiet time.

Some of the ways we can keep a prayerful attitude and heart is rejoicing always, giving thanks in every situation, singing praises, and voicing short prayers throughout the day. Having a prayerful heart and attitude keeps us mindful of God's presence and our total dependence on Him. If you are constantly thanking God, if you are constantly thinking about Him, you are likely to pray more frequently and spontaneously. As you spend more time with Him, your life and prayers will conform to His heart. Then you will begin to pray the will of the Father, and then you will see your desires granted. Through prayer, God places His desires into your heart, His desires become your desires, thus fulfilling **Psalm 37:4**—"Delight thyself also in the Lord, and He shall give thee the desire of thine heart." This will become your reality.

Prayer is not complicated, but it is powerful. The primary purpose of prayer is to nurture and grow our relationship with God. We are designed to have a relationship with our Heavenly Father. Just as God walked with Adam and Eve, it is God's desire to walk and talk with us in the cool of the day. As you can see, praying doesn't only have to occur on your knees—you can walk and pray. Reflect back to our definition of prayer—talking with God. You can talk to God at any time, at any place, with no restrictions! So far, can you see why prayer is your most powerful tool? In prayer, we exchange our fragility and weakness for God's supernatural power. Just being connected to our Sovereign God from whom all power flows is enough inspiration for me. But it gets better.

Prayer is the foundation for our armor. It ensures that the other pieces are tightly and securely fitted. Although it is not mentioned as one of the six pieces of spiritual armor mentioned in **Ephesians 6:11-18**, it is actually the catalyst of it; it activates the performance of everything else. Prayer is the foundation that holds everything else together. The Word of God tells us to "Submit to God, resist the Devil and he will flee" **(James 4:7).** Submit yourself to God in prayer. The armor was designed to protect you from the fiery darts of the Devil. But you must be covered in prayers before you even think about stepping out on the battlefield.

When studying the six pieces of armor, everything points to being clothed in Jesus; every piece of armor represents Jesus Christ and being clothed in His Righteousness. When you step out for battle, the Devil and his imps should see only Jesus, and no part of you should be exposed. Friend, Jesus is the only one that can and has defeated Satan. We are not a match for the Devil in the flesh. In order for God's armor to fully protect us, there must be an established relationship and a consistent line of communication between us and Heaven. This is called prayer! As you continue to communicate with God, He will reveal the tactics and strategy for battle.

A soldier or warrior does not go to battle without receiving commands from headquarters. And that is how it is within the Kingdom of God. It is unwise to go to battle without directions, a strategy and your armor. God has insight, foresight and knowledge of all the angles the enemy will attempt to attack. He knows how to defeat and destroy the enemy. Our God is mighty in battle and you need to have a talk with Him before you step out onto the battlefield.

I will tell you that every time you wake up and place your feet on the floor, you have entered the battlefield. If you decide to go to battle blind-sided, without instructions and directions from Heaven, you are likely to be wounded, defeated and/or destroyed.

WHY DO WE NEED TO PRAY?

As stated, our primary purpose of prayer is to grow and develop our relationship with God.

We were created in His image, for His pleasure, to bring honor and glory to His name. This is a summary of several scriptures combined to convey our purpose on earth. Therefore, in order to know your purpose—to bring God pleasure, honor and glory—you need to talk to Him to know what He likes. When you are in a marriage or relationship, you often talk to one another to see what makes them happy, what makes them sad, their likes and/or dislikes, and if you care about the person and the relationship, you will adjust your behavior or performance accordingly. If you do not care about the person or you're just not "feeling" them, you probably will not engage in extensive conversation with them or adjust your performance to please them. This same principle applies to the spiritual, relating to our Heavenly Father. The more time you spend with God, the more you will get to know Him. The more you know Him and about Him, the more you will begin to love Him, which will lead to obeying Him and aligning your desires to His desires. You will become more Heavenly-minded. You will gradually begin to abandon *your* ways and *your* thoughts and begin to surrender to His Lordship. God wants to have an intimate relationship with each of His children. Prayer gives that. God wants us to know the deep secrets of His heart.

You will never get to know the heart of God if you are not personal and intimate with Him.

If you are at a crossroad in your life and do not know what direction to take, if you need guidance with your spouse, job, career, children, ministry, or whatever crisis you may be facing today, you need to pray. Through prayer we gain all the treasures of God's wisdom and knowledge mentioned in **Colossians 2:3**. The Scriptures tell us that if any man lacks wisdom, let him ask of the Lord and He will freely give it to us **(James 1:5)**. Many of us are like the hamsters that keep running on the wheel and not going anywhere because we are not seeking God for His wisdom, knowledge, and direction. We are leaning on our own understanding or our own finite wisdom; in other words, worldly wisdom. God's wisdom is infinite, comprehensive, endless, limitless, never-ending and vast. He is an everlasting God; He is God from Beginning to Ending; He is all-knowing. Why would we not trust His knowledge? His ways and thoughts are so far greater than ours.

"In all thy ways acknowledge Him, and He shall direct thy paths" **(Proverbs 3:5)**. To acknowledge Him means you consult Him, you talk to Him about the path you should take; and then you wait for Him to answer. Know, my friend, that God cares about you, He cares about every area of your life, He is concerned with every detail of your life, no matter how insignificant you may think it is. He cares and wants you to talk to Him about it; remember, prayer is basically talking to God! If God knows the number of hairs on your head, you can trust and have confidence that our God is a caring God and cares about everything that concerns you—even what you should cook for dinner! Do not allow anyone to tell you something is not significant enough for you to talk to God about. If it concerns you, God is all ears! He is always listening and He is never too busy for His children.

Our prayer life is a strong indicator of the health of our relationship with God. A person's prayer life speaks volumes about their relationship with the Father; if you have a healthy prayer life, it will show in your lifestyle. You will be a fruit producer as defined in **Galatians 5:22-23;** "But the fruit of the Spirit is love, joy, peace, long-suffering, gentleness, goodness, faith, meekness, temperance: against such there is no law." Notice the first fruit of the spirit is love. You will begin to have love for God as well as humanity; this fulfills the two commandments Jesus gave us: "Love the Lord thy God with all thy heart, and with all thy soul, and with all thy mind [and] ... love thy neighbor as thyself" **(Matthew 22: 37, 39).** The more time you spend with Him, you will begin to take on His characteristics, because prayer aligns your heart with God's heart, placing you in a position to hear God's desires for you and have clarity and understanding to achieve His purpose in your life. As your love and relationship deepens for God, you will begin to see the world, situations, and circumstances as He does.

Prayer changes your perspective on how you view the world, your environment, yourself and your surroundings. You begin to see everything differently, because you are now viewing your environment through the lens of Jesus. Your spirit is seated in heavenly places, observing from a higher position *(Ephesians 2:6)*. For example, when you are in an airplane, or on a hill or mountaintop, everything appears small because you are elevated. Prayer keeps your heart and attitude in an elevated position. It keeps you focused on the greatness and power of God.

There is so much negativity in the world; we are surrounded by evil. Without prayer and renewing our minds with the Word of God, we can easily be conformed to this world's thought process. Jesus told us that we are in the world but not of the world **(John 17: 15-16).** It is the constant praying without ceasing that is going to keep our hearts and minds at perfect peace. Although we are in an evil perverse world, God gives us His power to resist temptation through prayer. As **1 Corinthian 10:13** tells us:

> There hath no temptation taken you but such as is common to man: but God is faithful, who will not suffer you to be tempted above that ye are able; but will with the temptation also make a way to escape, that ye may be able to bear it.

Prayer provides the strength to remain calm in the storm.

Quite often, we are focused on the temptation and until the last hour, most of us do not think about praying to God to reveal the way out. However, when prayer is a lifestyle for us, it is our first response to adverse situations, and we can be more confident and confront the temptation from a stance of victory. This passage of scripture lets us know that God has already made the way of escape before the temptation. Remember He is the God that knows your ending before the beginning. He may not reveal the escape plan at the onset of prayer, but you will have the confidence, peace and patience to wait for the outcome of His plan. You will not be so quick to take matters into your hands, or attempt to work things out yourself.

Wow, are you noticing all the God-like traits you are developing from praying? Confidence, peace, patience and self-control. The more you pray, the stronger your spirit becomes, and it will keep you from yielding to temptation. This was clearly illustrated in Jesus' temptation by satan in the desert and his spiritual agony in the garden of Gethsemane. The scriptures also tell us that Jesus was tempted at all points just as we are and yet he remained without sin **(Hebrews 4:15).** Where and how do you think He received the power and strength not to succumb to temptations? We will further discuss Jesus's temptations when we examine His prayer life.

We cannot escape the evil that is in the world today, but we can overcome it with a fierce, effective life of prayer.

REVELATIONS THROUGH PRAYING

Do you want to know more about God? Do you want to see His many attributes? Do you want to know God's plan and purpose for your life, your ministry, your family, your current situation? PRAY. God reveals Himself to us through prayer. God definitely has a plan for your life and it is a good plan with a great ending. In **Jeremiah 29:11** He tells us, "For I know the thoughts that I think toward you, saith the Lord, thoughts of peace, and not of evil, to give you an expected end." But how would you ever know God's thoughts and plan for you if you never communicate with Him? It is not by accident that in **Jeremiah 29:12** (the next verse after He tells us He has a plan), He tells us how to achieve those blessings: "Then shall ye call upon me, and ye shall go and pray unto me, and I will hearken unto you." Come on now, how clear can He make it? "I have a plan for you, I have the answer for what you are going through; I just need you to come and talk to me, so that I can give you insight and directions. Then you will not be confused about your life!" Wow, what an awesome God we serve! He is just waiting for us to make time to talk with Him. Friends, I do not know about you, but I can barely contain my excitement!

If this is not enough, in **Jeremiah 33:3**, the Lord tells us to "Call unto me, and I will answer thee, and show thee great and mighty things which thou knew not." If this is not enough incentive, God tells us in **Isaiah 65:24**, "Before they call, I will answer; and while they are yet speaking, I will hear." Wow! What is God saying to us? It is clear to me that God wants to reveal Himself to His children; this is God's invitation with open arms for us to come and sit at His feet and learn from Him. Friend, do you see how our God is bidding us to have fellowship with Him? We cannot begin to imagine how deeply our God loves us. This is the primary reason I believe the Holy Spirit inspired me to write this book about strengthening our relationship with God through prayer. God wants us to know Him, not just focus on getting a prayer answered. He wants us to know Him *intimately*.

An intimate relationship is defined as an interpersonal relationship that involves physical or emotional intimacy. Intimacy is characterized by passionate attachment. God wants us to be passionately attached to Him. He wants our emotions to be so connected to Him that we cannot imagine the thought of losing Him or being without Him. To be emotionally connected to someone means that the person controls your thoughts, your actions, your entire being. Isn't that what our all-knowing, all-powerful God wants? When we come to a place where God has total control, then we will begin to experience a greater revelation of who He is, and we will be able to trust Him with all the details of our lives.

There are so many scriptures in the Bible, in both the Old and New Testaments, that illustrate God's desire to reveal Himself to those who love Him, and the tools he uses to help Him. Let's take a close look at **1 Corinthians 2:10-11**: "... The Spirit searcheth all things, yea, the deep things of God. For what man knoweth the things of a man, save the spirit of man which is in him? Even so the things of God knoweth no man, but the Spirit of God." God is all-knowing; God is omniscient; He encompasses all knowledge of the universe, past, present and future. Not only did He create all knowledge, He *is* all knowledge. When we speak about the Spirit of God knowing all things, this surpasses our capacity to even imagine what God desires to reveal to us. Our perspective of God is so small, we don't even pray like we should. But trust me, our adversary knows how great and big our God is. The things of God, His secrets, His plans, the natural man has no knowledge of and cannot understand **(1 Corinthians 2:14).** When we pray, our spirit connects with the Holy Spirit which receives and delivers our messages to the Father. Then the Father through the Holy Spirit delivers the message to our spirit. Oh my goodness, I cannot emphasize this enough! God's Spirit searches the deep things of God; when you are in constant communication (prayer) with God, His Spirit will reveal to you the things that you need to know, He will reveal to you the direction you need to take. **1 Corinthians 2:12** tells us, "What we have received is not the spirit of the world, but the Spirit who is from God, so that we may understand what God has freely given us." God freely gives us insight, knowledge, and wisdom. There is no good thing that God will withhold from His children. All we have to do is ask Him with a sincere and loving heart.

God has provided us with His Holy Spirit, so we can clearly know and understand the things of God. We do not have to seek out worldly advice. The world or the natural man does not understand the things of God because the knowledge and wisdom of God is spiritually discerned, and only he that has the Spirit of God will understand the things of God. **1 Corinthians 2:13-14** goes on to tell us that once we have received wisdom from God's Spirit, then

[These] things also we speak, not in the words which man's wisdom teacheth, but which the Holy Ghost teacheth; comparing spiritual things with spiritual. But the natural man receiveth not the things of the Spirit of

God: for they are foolishness unto him: neither can he know them, because they are spiritually discerned.

This is important for us as believers of Jesus Christ, if we want to walk in the knowledge, power and wisdom of God. We spend so much time consulting others, confused about what direction we should take, walking aimlessly through life as if we have no purpose, when all we have to do is go to God in prayer. He desires to give us wisdom, directions, and instructions. This is such a profound passage of scripture as it relates to God's desire to lead us by His Spirit!

Imagine being taught by the omniscient God of the Universe! Imagine being taught by the Creator of the Universe; imagine all this knowledge and creativity being placed within you by the One that created knowledge, the One that created you and me. I do not know about you, Friend, but I want this! I get tired of hitting my head against a brick wall and not going anywhere. I get tired of running around in circles and ending up right back where I started. I get tired of throwing good money after bad, just because I have decided to do my own thing and not consult with the all-knowing God in prayer. **James 1:5** says: "If any of you lack wisdom, let him ask of God, that giveth to all men liberally, and upbraideth not; and it shall be given him." This is a promise, an assurance from our God, that we do not have to go through life blind without knowing our purpose or direction. And He will not get mad and blame us for not knowing what to do.

What are you waiting for? If you are facing a crisis today, if you are confused as to what you should be doing, if you need to make a decision regarding your career, family, ministry—seek God for wisdom that He graciously and generously gives to those who ask. God knows that we need Him for everything, and He is patiently waiting for us to realize that He is our Source. It is important that when we come to God in prayer, we empty ourselves of all our ideas and thoughts to allow God to pour Himself into us. This is one reason many do not see any changes after prayer: you are not emptying yourself and going before God totally naked. We must come to God with an unveiled mind and heart, so we can see and get to know God for who He really is.

Prayer shows God that you are totally dependent upon Him. It shows him that you are abandoning your ways, your thoughts, your intelligence, your self-reliance, and trusting in His power and wisdom. You are humbling yourself and acknowledging that you cannot move or do anything without Him. Humility begins with prayer; you will not seek someone for guidance, or directions, if you feel you do not need their help. When you pray, you are recognizing God's sovereignty, His omniscience and His power. Hopefully at this time, you can see how God reveals Himself to you in prayer. Hopefully, you can see that the more you pray, the more you will increase in revelation, knowledge, understanding and wisdom—not only in spiritual matters, but also in matters involving your everyday life. You will realize that you are more confident and at peace with matters concerning your family, job, career, education, marriage, health, ministry, business and every day-to-day crises. All because you decided to place your life in His hands through prayer.

The wisdom from God supersedes any worldly advice you will ever receive.

I hear so many believers express how perplexed and indecisive they are about their purpose, their situations and their lives. My first question is "How is your relationship with God?" You cannot have a relationship with God without prayer. I am not saying that you aren't saved. Many stop at salvation (accepting Jesus as Lord and Savior) but never take the next step in developing a relationship with Jesus or even becoming a disciple of Christ. Getting saved is the first step, and a very critical step; however, following Christ is a lifelong process. It is important to define your new relationship; exactly what does it mean to be in a relationship with God? There are several definitions for relationship; however, these are my favorites:

> Relationship: the state of being connected, joined together by a common bond. Alliance.

> *and*

> Relationship: the state of being connected by blood or marriage. (Are we not connected and joined to the Father by the blood of Jesus?)

Saying "I am in a relationship with God" is not a phrase that you loosely throw around without fully understanding what being in a relationship means. God is not Santa Claus, a genie, a
magician, or an errand boy that we can just run to when we are in need. No, Friend, He is much bigger than that and He requires more from us if we want to see our prayers answered. Praying is not only about us asking for things—it is about getting to know the One who created you and me. That is why this book focuses on building your relationship with God through prayer. God wants your heart. When He has your heart, then you will begin to experience Him in ways you never imagined. He gets your heart and you get His heart through prayer! I do not know about you, but I want God to look upon me and declare what He said about King David:

> I have found . . . a man after my own heart, which shall fulfill all my will. **(Acts 13:22)**

Except in my case, of course, it would be a woman rather than a man!

How will you know what God wants you to do? By spending time with Him in prayer. Not only will God reveal Himself to you, give you clarity on decisions, and define your purpose, He will also reveal areas in your life that may be a hindrance, sin or weakness. It is not to make you feel bad or condemned, it is to make you stronger and to not give any place to the devil. satan studies our lives and looks for areas where he can get in and cause havoc. Our God is a loving God, He is perfect and He wants to warn and protect us from all the schemes, tactics, wiles and devices of the Devil. Always look at God's corrections as redemptive and not punitive. God corrects those that He loves **(Hebrews 12-6).** However, if you do not comply and obey the correction, you could face an unanswered prayer situation. Once again, I am not saying that He doesn't love you or you are not saved—there may be some things that need to be addressed.

Friends, we have to always remember that we serve a Holy and Perfect God. Although He loves us with an everlasting love, His nature will not allow Him to tolerate sin. Therefore, we must be like David and maintain a repentant heart.

HINDRANCES FROM AN EFFECTIVE PRAYER LIFE

At this point we should know without a doubt that our Heavenly Father loves us, desires an intimate relationship with us, wants us to talk to Him, and not only does He hear our prayers, He answers them. I know some of you may be saying, not only are my prayers not getting answered, I do not think God even hears me! As stated earlier, the ears of the Lord are opened to the righteous **(Psalms 34:15).** However, there are times when we may have obstacles in our lives that will hinder or block God from answering our prayers. Let's remember and never forget that our God is holy, He's perfect, and He demands due reverence and respect at all times. Below are a few areas in our lives that, if not carefully monitored, addressed and surrendered unto the Lord, can become problems, and hinder if not stop our prayer life.

(1) Unconfessed Sin: If we tolerate or have unconfessed sin in our lives, it pushes God away from us and makes our prayers powerless. However, **1 John 1:9** tells us, "If we confess our sins, He is faithful and just to forgive us our sins, and to cleanse us from all unrighteousness." Look how merciful our God is—we do not have to continue in sin. That is why it is important to maintain a repentant heart.

(2) Lack of Faith: Without faith, prayer has no power **(James 1:6-8, Hebrew 11:6).** It takes faith to pray. You must believe

that the Creator to whom you are praying exists. You must believe that whatever you are asking, you will receive as long as you are praying according to His will. God sees your faith and responds to it.

(3) Disobedience: We must learn to obey God and His word. When God instructs us to do or not to do something, we must obey and act accordingly. This was evident with the children of Israel: because of their constant disobedience it took them longer to possess the Promised Land that was already guaranteed to them. This illustration can be seen in the books of Joshua and Judges. As it says in **1 Samuel 15:22**, obedience is better than sacrifice.

(4) Unforgiveness: We cannot enter God's presence with bitterness, hatred, and unforgiveness and expect God to bless us **(Matthew 6:14-15).** Just as Jesus forgave us and gave us a clean slate, He commands us to forgive those who may have wronged us—and there is no limit on how many times we should forgive them. If you have a problem forgiving someone, this is a good place to start in prayer; ask the Holy Spirit to give you the strength and power to forgive. God knows this may be challenging for you; that is why He sent the Holy Spirit to dwell within you to get you through these challenging situations.

(5) Wrong Motives: Sometimes we may have the wrong motive. **James 4:3** puts it bluntly: "Ye ask, and receive not, because ye ask amiss, that ye may consume it upon your lusts."

(6) Idols in our Lives: Obviously, today we are not worshipping bronze and molten calves. However, there are many things we turn into idols without realizing it. We must be careful that we are not placing anything before God. God demands that He is first in our lives. He will not take second place to anyone or anything. Modern day idols are money, cars, jobs,

family, spiritual leaders, education, ministries, clothes, and all forms of material possessions. Idol worship blocks your access to God **(Ezekiel 14:3).**

(7) Disregard for others: Prayer helps you become more compassionate towards others. It helps you to see others through the lens of Jesus; this seemingly unworthy person is a soul that He died for. You will begin to walk in love towards others. The more time you spend in His presence, the more you become like Christ. You will begin to take on His attributes.

(8) Unsurrendered Will: God promises to answer our prayers according to His will. The challenge is getting our will aligned with His will for our lives. That happens through prayer. **1 John 5:14-15** tells us: "And this is the confidence that we have in Him, that, if we ask any thing according to His will, He heareth us: and if we know that He hears us, whatsoever we ask, we know that we have the petitions that we desired of Him."

(9) Disregard for God's Sovereignty: Honor God; give Him total control of your life.

2 Chronicles 7:14 is a summation of all nine points: "If my people who are called by my name shall humble themselves, and pray, seek my face and turn from their wicked ways, then will I hear from heaven, and will forgive their sin and will heal their land." In this context "land" can symbolize you personally or a geographic area. In either case, your heart must be in the right position to receive healing. This is why the Lord wants the focus to be on strengthening our relationship with Him through prayer. As long as we maintain a repentant heart and keep our eyes on Jesus, satan is powerless over us. I am being redundant intentionally when it comes to the *repentant heart*. Having an unrepentant heart allows the Devil to gain entrance in our lives. And this entrance can and will allow our relationship with God to suffer, thus causing our prayers to go unanswered. We never want to be in a position outside of God's divine protection.

Reflection: Before we continue, now that you have a better understanding of prayer and the Father's heart desire to engage in fellowship with you, can you think of anything that may be hindering or blocking your access to the Father and preventing you from having an effective prayer life?

Prayer: Father, thank you for revealing to me the true meaning of prayer. Forgive me for not fully recognizing your desire to have an intimate relationship with me. Place within my heart a burning desire to draw close to you, so I can experience you in ways that I never thought possible. And Father, if there is anything in my life that has hindered my access to you, I ask that you reveal it to me, so I may address it and surrender it to your power. In Jesus name I pray, thank you and Amen.

VARIOUS METHODS AND TYPES OF PRAYER

Now that we have established the foundation for strengthening our relationship with prayer, let's examine the various types of prayers. Do you know what prayer to pray for what occasion? First, there is no right or wrong way to pray, as long as you are praying from the heart. However, the closer you get to God, the more intimate you will become with Him and the more you will have to talk to Him about. You will begin to see Him as your ultimate source—your friend.

Your prayers (communications) with Him will become longer and frequent. Not only will you pray without ceasing, you will be "praying always with all prayer and supplication in the Spirit, and watching thereunto with all perseverance and supplication for all saints" **(Ephesians 6:18).** You will begin to enjoy time alone with the Father, looking forward to adding variety and spice to your prayer life. Praying will no longer be frustrating, boring and tedious, because you have discovered the ultimate purpose to pray.

There are so many types of prayers and so many ways to communicate with your heavenly Father, which can add variety to your prayer life. You do not have to pray the same way every day; you do not have to use the same method of prayer. Prayer should not be a chore, something that you dread doing, mundane; this can lead to prayer becoming a ritual, legalism and empty religion. Just like human beings, God loves variety; look at the universe, look at each other! His marvelous handiwork throughout the earth reveals how He loves creativity and ingenuity, and He wants us to release that in our quiet times with Him.

If you are new to prayer, or just one who has a hard time getting started, many find the A.C.T.S. model an easy way to begin.

A= Adoration: Start out by praising God; He loves to be exalted and magnified. Tell Him how wonderful He is.

C= Confession: You always want to maintain a repentant heart. Confess any known sins or any deeds or thoughts that may have displeased the Father. You do not want anything between you that could hinder your access to the Father.

T= Thanksgivings: Always remember to thank God, because there is always something to be thankful for.

S= Supplications/Petitions: This is where you make your request known to Him.

I love the ACTS model, because it teaches us the importance of first adoring and uplifting God before we ask anything of Him. We are honoring Him; it sets the tone for a beautiful love relationship between you and the Father. Be mindful that you do not have to incorporate all the elements of this model in the same session. This is a framework to help get you focused and started toward praying.

As you mature and deepen your relationship with the Lord, the Holy Spirit will prompt you as to how and what to pray. You will notice that your prayers will shift focus from self to God and others. You will become more dependent on being led by the Holy Spirit, because the Spirit knows what we ought to pray. The more time you spend with the Lord in prayer, you will become more sensitive and attuned to His voice. This is how you learn to recognize the voice of God—by praying, and spending intimate and quality time with Him. There is no magic formula;

you have to spend time with Him in prayer and reading His Word. Below I have listed a few types of prayers with a brief description for each, to give you an idea of the various methods and types.

(1) Prayer of Agreement: Most of us have asked someone to be in agreement with us regarding a particular issue. The participants in this prayer circle must all be in agreement and believe that God is going to meet the requested need **(Matthew 18:19).**

(2) Prayer of Faith: This prayer is based on knowing with confidence that God hears you and will answer your prayer. You have this assurance because (1) you have faith that He exists; (2) you have been obedient in following His Word; and (3) you have prayed according to His will. You are now ready to stand steadfast on His promise that before you call, God will answer; while you are still speaking, God will hear **(Isaiah 65:24).** The key to this prayer is that you believe the moment you begin praying, not after you pray. God is not restricted to a timeframe and prayers have no expiration date; therefore, it doesn't matter when you see the result of your prayer, or how long it takes to manifest in the natural world; you know your God is faithful and has already answered the prayer in the Spirit realm. Your spiritual maturity has provided you with the understanding that as long as you pray according to His will and you met the other criteria, God immediately answered your prayer **(Isaiah 65:24, Daniel 10:10-24).** As with all prayers, it is your faith combined with God's power that will cause the answer to manifest in the physical realm.

(3) Prayer of Consecration and Dedication: Although this prayer can be done at any time, it is usually done when one is preparing for ministry, when you are seeking specific directions or instructions, or beginning to walk in your calling or purpose. With this prayer, you are totally surrendering yourself to the will of God; you are relinquishing your desires and your will in exchange for His desire and will for your life. You are allowing God to set your direction and make your decisions. This is probably the most challenging prayer type. A perfect example of this prayer is Jesus praying in the Garden of Gethsemane **(Luke 22:42):** "Father, if thou be willing, remove this cup from me; nevertheless not my will but thine be done." Notice, Jesus had His own will, and reading this scripture, He was a little hesitant about going through with the plan! But through an already established prayer life, He quickly abandoned His will and aligned Himself with the will of the Father. And we know that surrendering to the Father's will was not easy, because Scripture tells us that His sweat was like drops of blood! Friend, I do not know about you, but I can say that I've never prayed that hard!

(4) **Prayer of Praise and Worship:** This prayer type should always be incorporated into our prayers. We should worship, praise and bless God daily **(Psalms 145).** A praise and worship prayer is not asking for anything. You aren't seeking directions; you aren't seeking guidance. You are acknowledging Him for His greatness, and you are honoring and glorifying Him for all His marvelous work throughout the earth. This is an expression of love and adoration for and to God. The more you praise and worship God, the more you will see God giving you the desires of your heart, without your asking. You will find many examples of this type of prayer in the book of Psalms.

(5) **Intercession involves praying for others:** You are praying on behalf of someone or something else. As you grow in

the Lord, you will find yourself doing more of this type of prayer. Your vision has increased, because you are spending more time with the Father and you are taking on the things that are important to His heart. You will begin to see that souls and His creation are important to Him. You will be directed by the Spirit what to pray and how to pray. The Holy Spirit will make intercession for you **(Romans 8:26).** That is why it is important to pray daily in the Spirit. An excellent example of an intercession prayer is the Lord's prayer in **John 17:1-26**. (This extremely long prayer is not the "Lord's Prayer" you may have learned in Sunday School; take the time to look it up, for it is touching.)

(6) **Prayer of Binding and Loosening:** Jesus introduces this prayer to use in the Gospel of **Matthew 18: 18-19:** "Verily I say unto you, Whatsoever ye shall bind on earth shall be bound in heaven: and whatsoever ye shall loose on earth shall be loosed in heaven. Again I say unto you, That if two of you shall agree on earth as touching any thing that they shall ask, it shall be done for them of my Father which is in heaven." This is our warfare prayer. Jesus wants us to know that we have authority here on earth because of our covenant rights through him. When you place your faith in Jesus Christ, you have His power and authority to bind evil and loose God's plan, blessings and purpose in any situation. When we bind something, we are declaring it unlawful based on God's Word. Often in life we do encounter evil, and we must learn how to use our inherited authority to bind the evil forces involved; then we can loose or call forth God's plans for healing and restoration. Our faith in God's word releases the power from Heaven that binds the evil that we are facing on earth. And finally, like everything else in the Kingdom of God, binding and loosening must be in accordance with God's word.

Reflection: Now that we have a better understanding of the different types of prayer, which type do you mostly find yourself praying? Do you pray the same types of prayer all the time? In what ways do you think you can add variety to your prayer life?

Prayer: Father, thank you for teaching us how to pray; how to perfect our communication with you; and as a result, how to grow and mature in our prayer life so we can experience you in greater ways. Amen.

Thus far, we have learned that prayer is simply talking to God, and we can talk to God every day, all day. The more we talk to God, the more sensitive we become to hearing and recognizing His voice. This is praying without ceasing.

PRAYING IN THE HOLY SPIRIT

We cannot discuss prayer without mentioning praying in the Holy Spirit by using the gift of tongues (our heavenly prayer language). There is a difference in being sealed with the Holy Spirit (which all believers receive when they truly accept Christ) and being baptized with the Holy Spirit and with fire **(Acts 1:5).** This is what happened on the day of Pentecost. The believers in the Upper Room were baptized with the Holy Ghost and fire, as evidenced by speaking in other tongues. If you are a believer and have been baptized with the Holy Spirit, with the evidence of speaking in tongues, this is a gift from God to his children and I encourage you to use it to build up your spiritual self. If you have not been baptized with the Holy Spirit, and you are a born-again believer, this does not mean you were not sealed with the Holy Spirit when you accepted Christ.

Without going into depth about being baptized with the Holy Spirit, I will say that it is a free gift from God that He gives to His children for the asking, and He is still baptizing those who earnestly desire it with the Holy Spirit. Just ask Him.

The reason that this gift is so important is that it releases the mysteries of God, and ignites our hearts with passion for Him. Scriptures tell us that our God is a consuming fire, and that is what the Holy Spirit does—it keeps the fire burning for Jesus.

The ability to pray in the Holy Spirit is powerful and shows our spirit having direct communication with God's Throne Room. Our spirit should be constantly communicating with the Spirit of God, and this is one way that we can be assured that is occurring. As we communicate in the Spirit with God, His Spirit is always relaying information and directions to our spirit, which will lead us into all truth and righteousness.

The Holy Spirit makes intercession for us—it travails, it moans and groans—to get us through trials, tribulations and difficult times. The Holy Spirit always prays for the perfect will of God, He knows exactly what we ought to pray. That is because He is the third Person of the Trinity, and that is one of His roles—to intercede on our behalf. The groans and utterances may be beyond our comprehension, but trust me, Friend, they have meaning, and God knows exactly what each groan, each moan and each utterance means **(Romans 8)**.

There are times, when I go before the Lord, and I just do not know where to start praying. My heart may be heavy, or I may just be perplexed as to where to begin. This is where I begin to start praying in the Spirit. Suddenly, I will begin to experience God's strength and power consuming me. This is when I know my spirit has connected with the Throne Room. My voice gets stronger and more boisterous; I begin to feel bold and confident. And if I am facing conflict or dilemma at that time, I begin to feel inner peace. The Holy Spirit takes over and makes intercession on my behalf. He knows exactly what to pray for to get results and what I need at that time. Praying in the Spirit deepens your prayer life, it edifies you, and it sensitizes your heart to the things of the Holy Spirit **(Jude 1:20)**. To obtain a better understanding of praying in the Spirit and its benefits, read **Romans 8:26-27, Ephesians 6:18 and 1 Corinthians 14-1-19.**

OLD TESTAMENT PRAYING WARRIORS: JOSHUA, NEHEMIAH AND JABEZ

Now, we are going to direct our attention to some powerful, awesome warriors of God, including our fierce and powerful role model, Jesus Christ. At this point, I hope you realize and understand the power in prayer. Friend, I cannot emphasize enough—*do not underestimate the power of prayer!* When you make prayer your first choice, it shifts the battlefield to your favor. When the enemy comes in like a flood against you, do not get stressed out or overwhelmed, because you have already made your heavenly deposit of prayers—all you have to do is go into your heavenly bank account and make a withdrawal. Oh, what a wonderful feeling to know that you have enough prayers to cover whatever the Devil brings your way!

Let's take a look at how the power of God was displayed in and through the life of three Old Testament heroes. We are going to start this journey with Joshua.

Joshua

Joshua was a man of war. While Moses' assignment was to deliver the Israelites out of Egypt, Joshua's assignment was to take the Israelites into the Promised Land. Obviously, both were men of prayer. There is a lot to be said about Moses and his relationship with God, but for the sake of time, we are going to focus on Joshua. After the death of Moses, God commissioned Joshua to arise and take the people into the Promised Land **(Joshua 1-11-16).** God had given them the Promised Land forty years ago, so it should have been a piece of cake—just walk into it and possess it, right? No, our God is unpredictable, radical, powerful and loves to show how great He is. In order to get into the Promised Land, they had to get over the walls of Jericho. Jericho had fortified walls 25 feet high and 20 feet thick, with soldiers standing guard on the walls. Jericho was perceived as a city of military power and strength. It would have definitely taken a miracle to get these walls down. We know our God is a miracle worker and nothing is impossible for Him. Joshua, obviously, checked into Heaven for the strategy for this task.

God had specific, explicit details for Joshua in conquering the walls of Jericho. They may not have made sense, but Joshua obeyed—and the word of God tells us the walls came down by the power of God. Yes, God could have knocked the walls down; He's all powerful and He can do anything he wants, whenever He wants, But He chose to do it this way (1) so the Israelites could see where they were in their faith, (2) the people could see the value of obedience, and (3) so God could show His Power. Prayer shows your dependence on God for everything. It looks outside of yourself to the greatness of God.

Many times, we are going to have to fight for what God has already given us and that fight needs to begin on our knees in prayer. We are not fighting for victory; Jesus already gave us victory at the cross. We are fighting from a position of victory, to obtain and maintain what is already ours. God *had already given them the land;* they just had to be obedient and allow God to use them to destroy the enemies who were living there. The blueprint for the job was already provided.

God has already given us all things that pertain to life and godliness **(2 Peter 1:3)**. All we have to do is pull it down through fervent, persistent prayer. There are some things that will only be released through prayer. Let Thy will be done on Earth as it is in heaven!

Nehemiah

We cannot talk about Old Testament praying warriors without touching upon Nehemiah. Nehemiah was a Jewish leader who had a passion and love for God and the things of God. When he saw that Jerusalem was still in ruins after it was conquered and destroyed by the Babylonians in 586 BC, this grieved his heart, and he took it upon himself to do something about this devastation. Nehemiah sought God for the rebuilding of the walls of Jerusalem. To do this, he fasted and reached out to God in prayer. It is worth closely examining Nehemiah's prayer, and the elements that make this such a powerful one—a prayer that touched and moved the heart of God. Although the Bible records several of Nehemiah's prayers, we are only examining the prayer in Nehemiah, chapter 1.

Obviously, Nehemiah was a praying man and had a relationship with God. Nehemiah 1:5 begins:

"I beseech thee, O Lord God of heaven, the great and terrible God, that keepeth covenant and mercy for them that love him and observe his commandments ...

Praise: He begins with praise and adoration towards God. This is also how Jesus instructed us to pray and acknowledge God. Nehemiah identifies God's character as being faithful to keep His covenant with His people. Always begin your prayer by acknowledging God's greatness.

(v6a) Let thine ear now be attentive, and thine eyes open, that thou mayest hear the prayer of thy servant, which I pray before thee now, day and night, for the children of Israel thy servants...

Petition: We know that God hears and sees everything, but just in case, Nehemiah makes a specific request that God hear his prayer. We also see persistence in this prayer. He has been praying to God day and night. He is serious about what he is going to ask of God.

(v6b-7) Both my father's house and I have sinned. We have acted very corruptly against you, and have not kept the commandments, the statutes, nor the ordinances which You commanded and gave your servant Moses.

Confession/ Repentance: Nehemiah admits the sin of his family, himself and the Israelites. We too should always confess and repent when we go before God. We always want to make sure our hearts are in a position to freely receive from God and we do not want sin to interfere with God's perfect work in our lives.

(v8-9) "Remember, I beseech thee, the word that thou commanded thy servant Moses, Saying, if ye transgress, I will scatter you abroad among the nations: But if ye turn unto me, and keep my commandments, and do them; though some of you were cast out to the farthest part of the heavens, yet I will gather them there and bring them to the place which I have chosen.

Remind God of His Word: God knows His Word and His promises to us. Remind Him of His Word. This strengthens your faith and application of the Word.

> (v10-11) Now these are thy servants and thy people, whom thou hast redeemed by thy great power, and by thy strong hand. O Lord, I beseech thee, let now thine ear be attentive to the prayer of thy servant, and to the prayer of [all] thy servants, who desire to fear thy name: and prosper, I pray thee, thy servant this day, and grant him mercy . . .

Humility: Nehemiah acknowledges that the Israelites are servants, and they are totally dependent upon God's great power. Here again, he exalts God. Throughout our praying, we must continue to exalt God and reiterate His great attributes and character.

This is not a step-by-step instruction guide for praying. But I want to highlight the elements employed in this prayer, which are essential to any prayer. As we deepen our relationship with God through prayer, we will learn and become conscious of how to touch His heart.

Nehemiah begins and ends his prayer with praise and adoration to God. He reminds God of who the Israelites are and what they mean to Him (not that God forgot). But Nehemiah was interceding on behalf of his people, like Moses did. Remember, there isn't a right or wrong way to pray, an official or unofficial way to pray. God is looking for sincerity. I encourage you to prayerfully read the Book of Nehemiah and closely examine how he fervently sought after God and successfully rebuilt Jerusalem's walls in 52 days because of the intervention and power of God!

We see the power of prayer in the lives of Joshua and Nehemiah. God is still looking for people who would dare to believe and trust Him for the impossible. He has not stopped performing miracles, we have just stopped believing; therefore, we aren't sending up fervent, heartfelt prayers. We have allowed ourselves and our distractions to get in the way of seeking God for the impossible. In order to believe and see God do the impossible, you have to take yourself, your intellect, out of the equation. As already stated, prayer symbolizes humility and it lets God know that you are totally dependent upon Him.

Jabez

The third warrior we are going to look at had a very short but profound appearance in the Bible. We do not know much about him, because he is mentioned only once in Scripture, but his prayer was so powerful, it moved the heart of God and God granted him what he requested.

The person is Jabez, and his short story can be found in **1 Chronicles 4:9-10.** Jabez was not known for heroic feats, but he was known for his profound prayer. His prayer was short, direct and to the point. Let's look more closely at these four powerful phrases:

> Oh, that thou would bless me indeed, and enlarge my coast, and that thine hand might be with me, and that thou would keep me from evil, that it may not grieve me! **(1 Chronicles 4:10 KJV)**

And the Lord granted him the request. As we see, it is not about using big, long fancy words. Jabez's prayer was short and simple, but from the heart. The Lord wants to show us that it is not the quantity of our prayer, but it is the quality of the prayer. God is looking at the sincerity of our hearts.

This was an open-ended prayer; Jabez left it up to God how He would decide to "bless" him, because God knew what he needs. God knew what would be best for him. Your particular situation or circumstance will determine if you should have an open-ended prayer or a more specific prayer. Jabez knew he also needed God for favor and protection, all which was requested in his prayer.

I hope by now that your heart is hot, on fire and ready to strengthen your relationship with God through prayer. Needless, to say that there are countless Old and New Testament praying warriors that knew how to touch the heart of God with prayer. God is not looking for perfect people, because He knows that in ourselves, we cannot reach that standard of perfection. That is why we have Jesus; it is through Jesus that we have been made perfect and have been reconciled back to the Father, and it is through our prayer life that the reconciliation is identified, developed and perfected. Our heart must become an altar of prayer, that hungers and thirsts after God. "My soul thirsteth for God, for the living God" **(Psalms 42:2)**. This is when our soul yearns to continually see the face of the Lord.

In these last days, the Father is seeking mature men and women who are ready to go into battle and who are not fearful. God wants us to wholeheartedly seek Him. God wants His people to operate from a spiritual point of reference, as opposed to a physical point of reference. Let's remember that prayer doesn't change God; it changes *you*! It doesn't make God move any faster or do anything that He wasn't already going to do. It places us in a position to hear and receive from Heaven. In order to stand tall and know our position in Christ, we will need to have a strong, steady, unmovable relationship with Him. Prayer is our power source. We have to be connected to the Father, especially in these last days.

Who knew and understood more about being continuously connected to the Father than our Lord and Savior, Jesus Christ? Jesus is the perfect role model to emulate when it comes to developing our prayer life. Yes, I know that He was God, but He also was 100% man, meaning that He had to learn, prepare, grow and develop before He walked into His earthly ministry. Let's take a look at Jesus' prayer life.

OUR NEW TESTAMENT MODEL: JESUS

Praying Like Jesus

Prayer was a vital part of Jesus' life here on earth. He prayed regularly, passionately and fervently. When Jesus prayed, the heavens opened. Wow, imagine that! Jesus is our perfect example of how we ought to pray. If the Son of God found it necessary to stay connected to the Father, we must follow in His footsteps. Jesus faced all sorts of heartaches, trials, headaches, suffering, obstacles, temptations, and persecution, but He would not have been able to endure had He not been continuously connected to the Father. Jesus's life demonstrated that we should pray at all times about everything and anything.

Jesus prayed during events, He prayed short prayers, He prayed long prayers. He prayed in a variety of settings, He prayed in private and in public. He prayed in times of joy, in times of sorrow. He prayed for Himself, He prayed for others; in short, He prayed on *all* occasions. How often are we praying?

Our Lord and Savior was a praying sensation. That is why we cannot talk about prayer without closely looking at and examining the prayer life of Jesus. Let's take a closer look at when Jesus prayed and allow this to be our marker for an explosive, powerful, passionate prayer life.

When Jesus prayed, things got accomplished. The blind recovered their sight, the lame walked, the dead got up and demons fled in terror! This is what I am talking about: prayers that change things, prayers that move mountains. Prayers that open up Heaven—prayers that make a visible difference in the world. And this type of prayer is available to all of us. How badly do you want a prayer life like Jesus'? Well, you can have it, if you are willing to make sacrifices and spend quality time in the presence of the Father.

As we follow Jesus, we see that on numerous occasions He got away by himself to spend time in prayer with the Father. There are times that He spent the entire night praying. Friend, there isn't any shortcut to having a powerful prayer life, other than quality alone time with the Father. When you spend alone time with God, you are inviting and allowing Him to impart His attributes into you; that is how you will begin to take on Christ's characteristics. I am sure you have heard the saying, "the more you hang around someone, the more you begin to resemble them." How awesome it would be to look and talk like Jesus, and that is the will of the Father! We want Jesus to rub off on us! Then we will begin to see changes occur within our surroundings, environment and within ourselves.

Jesus Prayed Before Important Decisions: Luke 6:12-13

Jesus sought the Father before He made any important decisions. Unlike many of us, He didn't rush into making decisions. He didn't go off on His own and do what He wanted to do and then ask God to bless it! Jesus' decisions were already blessed before He made them, because He and the Father had already discussed the outcome. Remember, God knows the ending before the beginning. Therefore, if we seek Him first, many of our outcomes may be less devastating.

Choosing the twelve disciples was one of the first major decisions that Jesus had to make. Needless to say, the disciples were carefully and prayerfully chosen (just like you and I have been). In fact, **Luke 6:12-13** tells us that Jesus went off to the mountain to pray, and He spent the entire night in prayer to God. "...He went out into a mountain to pray, and continued all night in prayer to God. And when it was day, he called unto him his disciples: and of them he chose twelve, whom also he named apostles." Wow! *Jesus prayed all night*. Now remember, prayer is basically talking to God. So, looking at prayer in the light of talking to God, Jesus talked to God all night about the decision they had to make regarding the disciples. This doesn't necessarily mean that He was on His knees all night. But what it does mean is that He and the Father had a deep heart-to heart discussion. I can imagine Jesus and the Father at the mountain, maybe with a campfire going, roasting marshmallows, reviewing a list of potential candidates, listing the pros and cons, talking about the one who would betray Him, then finally, the Father made the final decision. Verse 13 tells us when day came, Jesus called His disciples and selected twelve of them. And the choice was a success! How often do we arbitrarily make decisions without consulting God? And then we say "the Lord told me," but we never really sought Him for His directions. We pay lip service to the idea that the steps of the righteous are ordered by the Lord, but God is nowhere in the equation when we make our decisions.

When we seek God before acting, our outcome will be successful. I am not saying that everything is going to be easy sailing and there will not be obstacles or struggles. It may not even look good to us, or be comfortable for us. But we can rest assured and have confidence that it *will* be good for us. Because the Word declares to us that "All things worketh together for good for them that love God, to them that are called according to His purpose" **(Romans 8:28)**. The fact that we are hungry and diligently seeking Him shows that we love Him. And this is illustrated by the way we actively and passionately pursue Him in prayer.

Jesus Prayed for Daily Guidance: Mark 1:35

Jesus arose early in the morning, before daybreak, went to a solitary place and prayed **(Mark 1:35)**. Jesus had face-time with God, before He faced the world. This is why He was always able to maintain His composure, His peace, and stability in all situations. Jesus received His daily assignments from the Throne, before He went out on the battlefield. In order for us to continually maintain our position of victory, we must have face time with God before we face our environment and surroundings. God equips us, gets us prepared for the daily task, conveys our daily assignments, provides us with peace, strength, endurance—in essence, His grace for that day's task. Jesus was able to heal the sick, open blind eyes, cast out demons, heal the lame and other miracles, because He sought the Father early in the morning. He only did what He saw the Father doing **(John 5:19)**. And, when did He see the Father doing all of this? Exactly, in His quiet alone time with the Father. The Father revealed to the Son who should be healed, who should receive sight, who should walk that day, where to go, what method to use. This type of direction, guidance, only comes by spending quality time with the Father.

Most of us have very busy schedules. We work, go to school, have to attend to the children, family, husband—and we just do not have time for a morning session with God. Friend, I encourage you to start by setting aside 10-15 minutes for prayer. Then, perhaps, you can begin to increase to 20-25 (in five-minute increments). You will be amazed at how much battleground you can cover in a fifteen-minute prayer. Remember, it is not about quantity, but quality time with the Father.

Jesus' disciples were so impressed by His prayer life and the way things changed when He prayed that in **Luke 11:1**, one of His disciples asked, "Lord teach us to pray." And the Lord gave us a model to approach the Father. This prayer is basic, but it covers every element we need to begin our journey to a successful prayer life. It establishes the foundation of entering into God's presence. From this foundation, you can begin to build and expound on your personal prayer life. Still following the prayer life of Jesus, let's take a closer look at these four profound verses in what is known as the **"Lord's Prayer."**

1st "Our Father which art in Heaven. Hallowed be thy name."

We are establishing our relationship with the Father—recognizing His holiness, reverencing Him, acknowledging that He is sacred and to be feared. The closer you become with God, the more you will relate to Him as your Father.

2nd "Thy Kingdom come, thy will be done on earth, as it is in Heaven."

This let us know that God has an established Kingdom where He rules and reigns; He is King! We are asking for God's Kingdom to rule and reign here on earth, as it is in Heaven. Some apply this to the coming of Jesus establishing His Kingdom on earth (the Second Coming of Christ); however, we are applying this passage of Scripture to us in history now. We want to release the power and will of God on earth today. Have you ever stopped and asked yourself what is it really like in Heaven? What am

I really asking God to release on earth and in my life? Take a moment to think about this.

3rd- "Give us this day our daily bread"

His grace is sufficient to meet our daily needs. That is why Scripture tells us not to worry; tomorrow will take care of itself. God is a "right now" God, and "I Am" is present tense. God wants us to focus on Him in the here and now. His grace is sufficient for whatever you need now. Don't get lost in tomorrow; God has already been *in* your tomorrow, so He already knows the outcome! Wow, what a mighty God we serve, who gives us the assurance that we do not have to worry about tomorrow, because He has already taken care of it. Please note, I am not saying we should not set goals. But be sure your goals align with and include God's plan for your life.

4th "And forgive us our debts, as we forgive our debtors."

This is a big one for many believers. Friend, if we want the Father to forgive us, we have to forgive others. I am not saying that it will be easy, but we have no choice in this matter. This is a major hindrance that will block your access to God. If you have a difficult time forgiving those who have hurt you, pray and ask God to help you *want* to forgive, and to give you the strength to do so. Be honest with the Lord and ask the Holy Spirit to help you in this area, because you can forgive if you want to. The Father's grace will enable you to forgive those who have hurt or mishandled you. Jesus tells us, if we do not forgive others, the Father will not forgive us. You have no choice; you have to forgive—no ifs, ands, or buts!

One of my favorite praying moments of Jesus was when He was in the Garden of Gethsemane. We know from studying the Scriptures that Jesus was going through deep mental and spiritual agony as he prayed there the night before His trial and crucifixion. How many of you have been in a place of mental or spiritual agony? All four Gospels provide a perspective, with slight variations, of Jesus in this dark hour. In order to see this account in its totality, I encourage you to read all four Gospels.

PRAYING TO RESIST TEMPTATION

There is so much in the Gospels about Jesus' prayer life, but what resonates with me is the way He prayed to resist temptation. This is where we see His humanity. He was sad, He felt alienated, His flesh was weakening in the face of the anguish that awaited Him. We also see that Jesus had His own will and that is evident when He states "Nevertheless, not what I will, but what thou wilt" **(Mark 14:36)**.

Carrying the sins of the entire world was not an easy task for the Lord to take on. His soul was exceedingly sorrowful unto death. Jesus could have easily decided that He didn't want to go through with this plan; He could have yielded unto temptation and said "Forget this!" Although His flesh had weakened at this point, His Spirit was strong, from continual and constant fellowship with the Father His entire earthly life. Jesus didn't just start praying this night. This shows us that yes, our flesh is going to get weak at times, but if we have a dynamic prayer life, the spirit will always overcome the flesh. However, this only happens when you constantly feed your spirit with the Word of God and prayer; then your spirit will be strong enough to resist temptation when it knocks at your door—and we all know that temptation is that unwanted, unwelcomed, uninvited pest!

Another important account in these passages of Scripture occurs in **Luke 22:40** when Jesus urged the disciples to pray that they enter not into temptation. And what did they do? They fell asleep! How many of us have purpose in our hearts that we are going to pray and then wake up thirty minutes later? Our intentions are good, we really want to pray, but as soon as we get on our knees or lie across the bed, our eyelids become heavy, we suddenly get exhausted, and no prayer! This is a trick of satan. As stated earlier, prayer is our most powerful weapon and of course, the Devil doesn't want us communicating with the Father to get the strength and power to destroy him and his tactics. Jesus told his followers that the spirit is willing, but the flesh is weak. And the Scriptures show us what happened with the disciples due to no prayer. Peter cut off a soldier's ear and denied Jesus three times **(John 18:10** and **Matthew 26:69-75)** and the other disciples scattered **(Mark 14:50).** I know all of these things had to happen, so that Old Testament prophecies could be fulfilled. But I can't help but wonder if the outcome would have been different or less painful had they prayed.

Thank God, Jesus had prayed for His disciples and us in **John 17:6-26.** He prayed that the Father would keep all those that were given to Jesus. This is an example of intercessory prayer. Jesus prayed that the Father would keep and sustain the disciples, and we see God's faithfulness in keeping them from being destroyed. The Roman soldiers could have easily killed them as well, but the power of prayer intercepted the Devil's plan. Friend, this is what happens when we pray! Whatever the Devil meant to use to destroy us is blocked by God, and we escape with minor irritations compared to what could have been devastating. Prayer doesn't necessarily stop bad things from occurring, but it can minimize its impact and or change our response to the situation. It will strengthen us to endure and press our way through to the other side. This is where God shows His strength in our weakness. We clearly see this illustrated in the Garden of Gethsemane with Jesus.

As already stated and revealed in Scripture, we see Jesus as the Son of Man; we see Him as 100% human. He agonized over the task that was set before Him. I love the fact that Jesus in his humanity showed us how to resist temptation with prayer. We see Jesus going through all the emotions and feelings that we go through when we are in despair. But how many of us have been so extremely distressed about something that our sweat was like drops of blood? This is an example of severe mental and physical pain our Lord suffered. This is some serious temptation!

But the lesson to be learned is how to overcome temptation by surrendering your will to the Father's will. And that is with fervent prayer. **Luke 22:43** shows us how an angel from heaven came to strengthen Jesus to continue in the will of God. And thank God for Jesus choosing to pray! That is why you and I are here today, because He chose God's way. The prayer didn't stop Him from going to the cross (it was not supposed to), but it gave Him the strength and power to resist the temptation to say "No—I changed my mind; I am not going to take on the sins of the world; let satan continue to rule the earth." That is exactly what the Devil wanted: for Jesus to submit to His own fleshly desires and will. But then he prayed. Jesus endured the cross, because He saw you and me on the other side. Prayer widens our vision so we can see beyond what is in front of us. Jesus saw beyond the cross.

I stress that this was done in His humanity, which means you and I can resist temptation through prayer too. Because of the Christ in us, we have the power, control and ability to continue in God's will and purpose for our lives. Next time you are tempted to give in or respond in a way that is contrary to the will of God, think about Jesus in the Garden of Gethsemane. Think about the agony, the despair, the anguish, the sweat that appeared as drops of blood. Through all of this, He prayed—and the Father heard, responded and sent reinforcement for Jesus to continue pursuing the will and purpose of God. And God will do the same for you and me.

As stated in the beginning, the purpose of this book is to strengthen our relationship with God through prayer. That is exactly the example Jesus shows us. Yes, He was 100% God, but as the Son of Man, He had to grow in His relationship with the Father. And as **Luke 2:52** tells us, "Jesus increased in wisdom and in favor with God and man." That should be our focus, to grow in our relationship with the Father, and not just look to God as our personal Santa Claus. These illustrations just touch the surface of Jesus's prayer life and are not intended to be a comprehensive picture of it. But I hope that you are able to glean from these illustrations how important it is to stay in continual communication with the Father. No matter how great you may think you are, you still need God's intervention and power for everything.

Prayer shows God that we are dependent upon Him. If our Lord and Savior saw the importance of showing God His dependence, to me, that speaks volumes on the importance of prayer. And, remember, it is not you doing all the talking! You are allowing God to speak to your heart and then obeying His instructions.

Reflection: Now that you see that there are many exciting ways to approach God, has this helped to increase your desire to seek Him, to want to see His face? What will you begin to do differently?

Prayer: Father, thank you for showing me how wonderful it is to spend quiet time with you. It is my heart's desire to be like Jesus. Teach me to pray in a way that will bring forth results that are pleasing and honoring to You. In Jesus' name, Amen.

Well, at this point, I know you are excited and can't wait to begin a passionate prayer life with your heavenly Father. You may still be asking yourself, "Where do I begin? I do not sound like the pastor, the prayer warriors, or Sister Jones. How do I put phrases and sentences together to begin praying?" Remember in the beginning, I said prayer is simply talking to God in your own words. Do not attempt to memorize others' prayers, and do not try to emulate others (unless it is Jesus); this is about speaking to God from your heart. Tell Him what is on your heart; tell Him about what you are feeling. There is no correct or incorrect way to pray. It is about your heart posture, your sincerity and reverence to the Father. God is seeking a pure and sincere heart.

WAYS TO START MY FERVENT PRAYER LIFE

The first segment of this book focused on the definition of prayer; the importance of prayer; different styles of praying; and frameworks for praying. The second segment of this book will focus on the mechanics of praying—where to start; how to start; and how to develop an intentional, deliberate praying strategy to connect to our Father through His Son Jesus, every single day. This is where we begin to establish a loving intimate relationship with our Heavenly Father. Recall, the purpose of this book is to strengthen our relationship with God through prayer. Prayer draws us close to God; it ushers us into His presence. **James 4:8** admonishes us to draw near to God; and what better way can we draw near to God than by entering into His presence with adoration? As a parent or spouse, how does it make you feel when your child or loved one approaches you with words of love, adoring you, telling you how beautiful or handsome you are, and saying you are the best mom, dad, husband or wife? It makes you feel good, and some of our loved ones really know how to put it on thick! So, imagine how God feels, when we enter into His praise exalting Him, letting Him know how wonderful He is—and doing this before we ask for anything!

Regardless of what type of prayer you are praying, what time of day you are praying, begin by magnifying the Lord. Exalt God for who He is, for all His greatness, awesomeness and holiness. This segment of prayer is all about God; the more you get to know Him, the more you understand His attributes and character, the more you will be able to praise and adore Him.

> **Example: God, You are the strong and mighty Creator; the entire universe declares your glory and greatness. You are Adonai, master of all, in control of everything; everything is under Your power and authority, and with this I acknowledge Your greatness. For You are the great I AM, You are everything that I need, when I need it, and because of this I am sufficient in all things.**

Starting out by praising God builds your strength, spirit and faith in Him. It sets the tone for everything else you may want to bring before His throne. The amount of time you spend in this prayer segment is determined by the time frame you are working with. You may also want to give God thanks along with the adoration, considering that we have so much to be thankful for. You can find examples of both adoration and thanksgiving in the book of Psalms.

After you extolled God and thanked Him, you want to make sure that there isn't any unconfessed sin in your life—anything that will hinder or break your fellowship with the Father. I know that I am being redundant—I covered this early on—however, this redundancy is intentional. I want it to penetrate deep into your spirit, how we must always maintain a repentant heart before the Father. Anything less is a sin of pride and we know how God feels about pride.

> **Example: Father, I repent of every action, deed, and thought that has displeased You, and I ask You to forgive and cleanse me with the pure and precious**

blood of Jesus. Father, search my heart, uproot anything and everything that distresses You and will hinder my fellowship with You. Father, create in me a clean heart so I may continually enjoy a harmonious fellowship with You.

If you are aware of a specific sin that you want to confess and repent of, this is the time and place to do that. Remember, that God is just and He will forgive and cleanse us of all sins and unrighteousness **(1 John 1-9).** We are not only speaking about what we label as "big sins"— we are referring to anything in our heart that is displeasing to God! That is why we ask Him to search our heart. Scriptures that relate to Prayers of Confession and Repentance can be found in **James 5:16, 1 John 1:9, Acts 3:19, Proverbs 28: 13, Psalms 32: 5.**

We enter God's presence with praise, thanksgiving, confession and repentance, because when we make our request to God, we don't want our request to be earthbound—meaning it isn't elevating to God's ears. We need to uproot and clear out those things to make a clear path to the Throne Room.

Talk to God as you would talk to a close friend; tell Him about your day; trust me, He cares about every detail of your life. If this is a morning prayer, ask Him for guidance; ask Him for strength and wisdom to complete your daily assignments and tasks. Ask God to take authority over your day, and to command all forces and elements to align with God's purpose and plans for you. You may want to start your morning with a song unto the Lord. Begin your day by saturating the atmosphere with praise that will bring down His presence. If you cannot think of anything to do in your morning worship, spend that entire time praising and thanking God; do not ask for anything, just adore Him for His greatness, for who He is.

Let Him know how much you love Him, how much you need Him!

You will be amazed at what praising God will do for your spirit! It will invigorate your entire day. You will begin to experience the presence and peace of God throughout your day, all because you set aside time to *woo* the Father! Face-timing the Lord at the beginning of your day will give you the strength and tenacity to conquer everything that is set before you. I am not saying that you will not experience struggles or challenges, but you will have the inner strength, peace and power to rise above the situation, see it through the lens of Jesus, and approach it with the guidance and wisdom of the Holy Spirit. Begin to make a habit to reflect on God's goodness early in the morning. Friend, we complicate prayer; our Heavenly Father never intended for it to be a difficult task to talk to Him. How about starting your morning out with a simple "Good morning, Father"? I know that you have a busy schedule, but you have to begin to make time for the One who gave you life! I challenge you for the next seven days: start your day with short praise like the one below. I used seven days (a week) as a starting point, because this should give you enough time to establish your morning prayer time.

> **Example: Good morning, Father, thank you for watching over me and my family throughout the night. Thank you for allowing me another opportunity to serve You, to love You, to obey You. You are truly worthy of all my praise; the entire universe declares Your glory and how awesome, wise and magnificent You are. You hold the world together with the power of Your hand; nothing is impossible for You. I look forward to this day, because I have the Everlasting God, the Awesome Creator,**

indwelling my spirit. You are my life, You are everything to me. I seal this praise in Jesus' name. Amen.

or

Good morning, my loving, merciful, compassionate, faithful and all-knowing Father. It is always a pleasure to awake in Your presence to behold Your goodness and beauty. This day shall be an awesome, blessed wonderful day, because I am walking with the Creator, the Master of the Universe, and all things are under Your authority and control. In Jesus' name, Amen.

There are so many ways to start your day with prayer; please get creative with your prayer life! God loves variety! If you like to sing, sing praises to Him. The Scriptures let us know that we can come into His presence by singing. Make up a melody in your heart. Remember, prayer does not have to be boring, tedious, a chore, or dreadful. God isn't boring and the closer you get to Him, you will see just how exciting He is!

After you have set the tone for your day with morning prayer, continue to think on things that are good, pure, admirable, honest, and virtuous **(Philippians 4:8)** as you proceed throughout your day. This will help you keep your thought process occupied with God and the things of God. You can silently give thanks and praise, or talk to God in your heart all day long. If you are faced with a complex or challenging task, whether it be work, ministry, or school-related, talk to God about it. Seek God for guidance; remember that is what our Lord Jesus did. "Trust in the Lord with all thine heart and lean not unto your own understanding; in all your ways acknowledge Him and He shall direct your path" **(Proverbs 3:5-6).** Do not sleep on this promise or think that it is something nice to quote; but really do seek God for guidance. This is a part of my daily prayer. I do not trust my finite knowledge or understanding on any subject. Friend, I have come to totally rely on the infinite, vast knowledge of my God. I realize that His resources, wisdom and connections are far greater than mine. I encourage you to begin to incorporate **Proverbs 3:5-6** into your prayer arsenal. Here is a short prayer for guidance:

> **Example: Father, because You are the all-knowing, powerful God, full of wisdom, I am standing on Proverbs 3:5-6; I am trusting You with all my heart. I believe that You will direct my path concerning this situation. I pray that You release your wisdom and Your ingenuity into my spirit so I may approach and respond in a way that is pleasing to You and will bring honor and glory to Your name. Amen.**

or

> **Father, release in me Your wisdom and knowledge concerning this situation. In Jesus' name, Amen.**

As we see, it is not the length of the prayer, it is not about the location, but the sincerity of the heart. It's about establishing our relationship through prayer. This is praying at all times without ceasing—always having our heart and mind in constant connection with the Father. These are segments of prayers to be prayed throughout the day. These are not intended to substitute for our one-on-one intimate time with the Father, but hopefully to enhance that time, because you were constantly thinking about and talking to Him. Obviously, everyone is not going to have the same schedule for their quiet intimate time. Although I do my morning prayers, evenings work best for me when it comes to the quiet, more relaxed and intimate settings. Once again, there is not a good or bad time when you choose to spend your quiet time with the Lord, just as long as you spend time with Him. Mornings work best for some, afternoons for others and then there are those late birds, like myself, where evenings and nights are more conducive to our schedules.

WAYS TO GET CREATIVE AND DEEPEN YOUR TALKS WITH GOD

Variety, variety—creativity, creativity. Think about yourself; do you like the same food, cooked the same way every day? That is how God is. He loves variety! We have been invited to fellowship, to talk with the Creator of the Universe! Ask Him to release His creativity in you to adore Him and fellowship with Him the way He desires. There are so many ways to enter His presence and approach His throne (but remember to be respectful). You do not have to approach God the same way every time. Below is a suggested list of creative ways to talk to God (pray).

(1) Prayer Walk: If you are a walker, put on your tennis shoes and do a prayer walk. Walk and talk to God! Talk to Him about your day, recite scriptures, tell Him what's on your heart, get to know what's on *His* heart. You will be amazed at how fun and exciting walking can become.

(2) Journalizing: Write your prayers down, then read them back to the Father. You do not have to memorize every prayer. This will not only enhance your communication; it will help you remember God's promises to you and help you stand securely on His Word. It will also help you structure and increase your prayer language. For example, when you are about to take on an uneasy task, you may pray **Exodus 33:14** like this.

Father, I stand on the promise that you gave Moses and the Israelites, "My Presence will go with you and I will give you rest." I rest in You, knowing that all things will work together for my good, because You are with me.

Journalizing helps construct and put sentences together for your prayers. As you read the passages back to God, in your quiet time with Him, you are building your prayer vocabulary.

(3)   Write a Poem: If you like poetry, so does the Father! God's admiration for poetry is evident in the five poetic books of the Bible, which are Job, Psalms, Proverbs, Ecclesiastes, and the Songs of Solomon. Write the poem and during quiet time, read the poem to Him. Remember, this is talking to God, and that is exactly what prayer is, *talking to the Father* in your language.

(4)   Write a Song: Just like you can pray the Scriptures, you can also sing the Scriptures—and our God loves music and singing. So, if you are one that enjoys singing, our Heavenly Father can't wait to make sweet melodies with you!

(5)   Write a Love Letter: Who doesn't enjoy receiving a love letter from their significant other? Trust me, Friend, God is no different. He loves it when we take the time to write Him a love letter from our heart, expressing our love for Him. Then read it to Him. Wow! Talk about an intimate connection! This will definitely bring a smile to His face. The love letter should focus on Him, His greatness, how much He means to you! This will really get a fire started between you and the Father!

(6)   Get a Prayer Partner: God didn't create us to be lone rangers. We all need someone we can trust enough to connect with in prayer. However, I do not suggest that this should be your

only time of prayer; you always need quiet alone time with the Father. One of the benefits of having a prayer partner is holding each other accountable to pray.

(7) Monthly Calendar: Make yourself a monthly calendar, outlining the topics or areas you want to focus on for that month. This will assist you in structuring and organizing your prayer life to ensure that you are covering in prayer all areas and aspects that need to be covered.

(8) Daily Prayer Themes: You can set daily prayer themes to upgrade your prayer life. This way you will not fall into the habit of praying for the same thing every day or run out of things to pray for. Using a different theme will also add variety and enable you to cover more areas and topics. A theme prayer schedule may look something like:

Sunday: Pray for the body of Christ and all spiritual leaders
Monday: Pray for family members and restoration
Tuesday: Pray for all political and civic leaders, our nation
Wednesday: Pray for youth, schools
Thursday: Pray for your city, community, and neighborhood
Friday: Pray for peace
Saturday: Pray for protection

These are just a few of the ways you can switch up your prayer life. As you begin using the theme method, you will come up with many themes to add to your prayer list. You will realize that there is so much in this world to pray about, and you will be on your way to "praying without ceasing." This shows you that prayer doesn't have to be mundane and tedious. I am sure you can come up with your own creative list. Take your prayer life outside the box and allow God to use your imagination to explore innovative ways to pray! Before you know it, you will have that vibrant and fierce prayer life that will shift and change your atmosphere, your environment and your surroundings. When you pray, things will happen. Not because of you, but because you have connected to the Power Source and you know who you are and to whom you belong! Amen!

As you draw close to God through prayer, you will begin to see and experience life through the eyes and person of Jesus Christ. You will become determined to fulfill your purpose and destiny. You will realize that God is on your side. He is your biggest cheerleader and He desires for you to succeed in everything that you do. But this can only occur when you are connected and in fellowship with the Father through Jesus Christ.

Because of the finished work of Jesus, we can boldly approach the Throne and talk to our Heavenly Father! What are you waiting for? Make the decision today to take your relationship with our Heavenly Father to the next level through our Lord and Savior Jesus Christ!

CONCLUSION

Friend, the goal of this book was to point, connect and strengthen your relationship with our Lord through prayer. The Father's most heartfelt desire is to enjoy a harmonious, loving relationship with His children. Prayer is that tool that God gave us to enter into His most holy presence. Once we understand that prayer is not only about asking God for things for ourselves, or focusing on our needs, but it is a privilege to be invited to talk with the Creator of the Universe, we gain a different perspective and appreciation for prayer. Prayer should never be an afterthought; it should always be our first reaction to any situation. Once we begin to realize what prayer does and how powerful it is, we will begin to pray without ceasing. Prayer will become our way of life and our spirit will begin to crave fellowship and communication with our Father.

Remember, prayer does not change God, but it changes you. It aligns your spirit with the spirit, will and purpose of God. Having fellowship with God is the heart of praying. We were designed to have fellowship with our Heavenly Father (this goes back to the Garden of Eden, Adam and Eve) and prayer develops our relationship with God and shows Him that we trust Him and are totally dependent upon Him.

Yes, God responds to the prayer of His children; however, God wants His children to perceive and relate to Him other than as a "gimme gimme" man! He wants a relationship with you and me! It is my prayer that everyone who reads this book is encouraged and inspired to seek God in ways that they had never imagined. I pray that the Holy Spirit will burn your hearts with fire for God and your desire for Him will intensify until nothing else matters but pleasing Him!

I pray God's peace and blessing upon every reader of this book!

PRAYER OF REPENTANCE AND SALVATION

You are saved by faith in Jesus Christ! Everyone who calls upon the name of the Lord shall be saved **(Romans 10:13)**. If you desire to come into the Family of God and become a joint heir with Jesus, confess with your mouth and believe in your heart the following prayer:

> **Father, I come to you through your Son Jesus Christ, who died for my sins. I acknowledge that I am a sinner, and need to be forgiven of my sin, I must acknowledge and believe in my heart and confess with my mouth that Jesus shed his blood, died on the cross and rose on the third day, so I may be cleansed, forgiven of all sin, past, present and future, and enjoy eternal life with You. Lord Jesus, I ask you to forgive me of all sin, I surrender my life to You as my Lord and Savior. From this day forward, I am now a child of God and a citizen of your Heavenly Kingdom. Amen.**

If you are new to the Family of Faith and want more information about salvation, forgiveness, and repentance, you should read the following scriptures: **Romans 9:10, Romans 3:23, Matthew 19:25-26** and **Philippians 3:4-11**. These are just a few scriptures to assist you with understanding your new faith.

The salvation process is just the beginning of a lifelong walk with Jesus. You do not want to stop at this process, because it is the best decision you have ever made.

Now you want to commit to discipleship. I encourage you to find yourself a good Word-teaching church and begin to associate with like-minded Christians so you can grow in your relationship with Christ.

May God bless you and increase you in the knowledge and understanding of our Lord and Savior Jesus Christ!

SUGGESTED PRAYING TOPICS

Pray for increased desire for and knowledge of God
Pray souls into the Kingdom
Pray for family members
Pray for restoration and healing for family members
Pray for your household
Pray for your children and their friends
Pray for our youth
Pray for our educators, school systems and all educational administrators
Pray for our nation, our President and all elected authorities
Pray for the judges and the judicial system
Pray for the Body of Christ
Pray for all spiritual leaders
Pray for those believers who are persecuted for Christ
Pray for unity among the saints
Pray for all civic leaders
Pray for Israel
Pray for confidence and boldness to proclaim the Gospel
Pray for your co-workers
Pray for your city, your community, your neighborhood
Pray for spiritual wisdom in all your affairs
Pray for your church
Pray for guidance
Pray for your deliverance as well as others

Pray for businesses and the economy
Pray for the arts, entertainment and the media sector

And the list goes on! This list by no means is intended to be exhaustive, but to provide you with some ideas and concerns to take to God in prayer. As you go through your day, ask the Lord to place things on your heart that you should pray about.

There may be times when you run out of things to pray for, or you may think that you do not have enough to talk to God about. There is so much that we need and should be taking to the Lord in prayer; and below are some suggested Praying Topics to help you begin your journey to praying at all times for all things!

REVIEW REQUESTED:

We'd like to know if you enjoyed the book.
Please consider leaving a review on the platform
from which you purchased the book.